A Map of the Night

A Map of the Night

Poems by

David Wagoner

University of Illinois Press
Urbana and Chicago

∞ This book is printed on acid-free paper.

Library of Congress Cataloging-in-Publication Data
Wagoner, David.
A map of the night : poems / by David Wagoner.
p.   cm.
ISBN-13: 978-0-252-03314-8 (cl. : alk. paper)
ISBN-10: 0-252-03314-0 (cl. : alk. paper)
ISBN-13: 978-0-252-07567-4 (pbk. : alk. paper)
ISBN-10: 0-252-07567-6 (pbk. : alk. paper)
I. Title.
PS3545.A345M37   2008
811'.54—dc22   2007052551

Acknowledgments

Grateful acknowledgment is made to the following publications in which the poems in this book were originally printed.

AGNI: "Blind Instinct," "The Center of Gravity," "The Heart of the Forest," "Desire"

American Scholar: "A Congo Funeral"

Atlantic Monthly: "A Snap Quiz in Body Language"

Bat City Review: "The Old Men"

Chariton Review: "What to Do All Day," "Watching a Boa Constrictor Yawn"

Cincinnati Review: "On Deck"

Connecticut Poetry Review: "Night Reconnaissance," "Moving through Smoke," "On Being Asked by the Assistant to the Governor of the State of Washington for an Appropriate Quotation from a Native American to Conclude an Inaugural Speech," "Upstream," "Looking Respectable," "On First Looking through the Wrong End of a Telescope," "The Heaven of Actors," "Weeds"

Crazyhorse: "The Elephant's Graveyard," "Meadowlark"

88: "Falling Behind"

Five Points: "In the Green Room," "At the Deep End of the Public Pool," "An Old Man Sitting Down," "An Assignment for Senior Citizens"

Georgia Review: "The Stand-up Cell"

Gettysburg Review: "Stopping along the Way"

Greatcoat: "Cemetery Grass"

Green Mountain Review: "In the Emergency Room," "Knots"

Hampden-Sydney Review: "What Do I Know?" "Passing the Road Gang," "Attention," "At Ease," "Unarmed Combat"

Hanging Loose: "A Lesson from a Student," "Elegy for a Safety Man," "Up against the Sea," "The First Touch," "For a Man Who Wrote *Cunt* on a Motel Bathroom Mirror," "The Moth"

Hotel Amerika: "Cell Division," "Changing Rooms," "What the Stones Say"

Hudson Review: "My Mother's Poem," "An Assignment for Student Playwrights," "In Youngs Creek," "Owning a Creek," "The Spider's Eye," "Between Neighbors," "On a Glass of Ale under a Reading Lamp," "An Informal Elegy for Neckties"

Long Journey: "Thoreau and the Quagmire"

Margie: "Being Taken for a Ride," "The Driver," "The Follower," "Curtsy," "Homework in Social Studies," "At the Scene of Another Crime"

Michigan Quarterly Review: "Thoreau and the Mud Turtle," "The Presumption of Death"

Mid-American Review: "The First Movie," "The Right Way"

New Republic: "For the Man Who Taught Tricks to Owls"

North American Review: "A Pastoral Elegy for a Pasture"

Northwest Review: "Catfish"

On Earth: "By a Pond," "Letting the Grass Grow under Your Feet"

Ontario Review: "Mr. Bones," "The Escaped Gorilla"

Pleiades: "Fighting the Blizzard"

Ploughshares: "Night Song from the Apartment Below"

Poet Lore: "Stakeout," "That Bird"

Poetry: "The Fan Dance," "Castle," "For an Old Woman at the Gate"

Poetry Flash: "Whistler's Mother"

Prairie Schooner: "A Visitor Calls on Joseph Conrad," "What the Houses Were Like Then," "On an Island," "The Other House"

Rhino: "Crane Fly"

Salmagundi: "What Billy Graham Said to Me at the Fair," "Under Fire"

Seattle Review: "My Snake," "An Old Man Stacking Firewood"

Shenandoah: "How Johnny Nolan Rescued Me"

Southern Review: "Judging a Hog"

Southwest Review: "The Hero," "Free Fall"

Sou'wester: "My Father's Dance," "Rescue"

Threepenny Review: "The Invitation"

Triquarterly: "The Solution to Yesterday's Puzzle," "The Red Hat"

Witness: "The Hunters"

Yale Review: "The Eve of the Festival of Venus," "Man Overboard," "Trying to Write a Poem While the Couple in the Apartment Overhead Make Love," "The Day I Believed in God"

Zyzzyva: "In the Graveyard of Major Appliances"

These are all for Robin, Alexandra, and Addy with love.

Contents

1

My Mother's Poem

Redwing blackbird, sitting on a stalk,
What would you say if you could talk?

She showed it to me shyly
after I'd been away for a long time.
She said this was the only one
she'd ever tried to write, and of course
it was only the beginning.

She'd written it on her own stationery
with an anonymous pastel flower
in the upper right-hand corner.
I'd seen it often before. My father
had never needed his own.

She said she couldn't quite decide
what to say next. She wasn't sure
how it should go on or maybe
it shouldn't, and she was showing me
because I was supposed to know about poems.

We stood there together
by the kitchen sink, looking out the window
at the swamp for a moment, both of us
wondering how to be inspired
in spite of feeling maybe it didn't matter

to anyone except ourselves
who could both see those birds hanging on
sideways to cattail stalks and singing
the one song they seemed to be sure of,
already knowing the end and the answer.

The First Movie

I walked with Jessamine, the tall black lady
who did our dishes, all the way downhill
to my first movie because my mother and father
were playing cards with Presbyterians.

We bought two tickets and ate our popcorn balls
while Tom Mix wore a hat and jumped off a horse
and shot white smoke at the bad men who shot back.
He was so important and huge, I believed in him.

I explained to Jessamine all the way uphill
what he'd been doing and why, and she said, *Yes,*
yes, that's right, while I explained his boots
and where the white horse slept and why he was wearing

a badge and those funny pants, and up the steps
and into the living room, I started explaining
to people sitting at tables what had happened
in the dark, how wonderful it had been

to see horses and ropes. So many words
came out of my mouth, they bumped into each other
and wouldn't fit the pictures I still saw
across the back of my mind. The people stared.

They sat across from each other, holding their cards
close to their chests like little fans and trying
not to laugh, but laughing anyway
and eating peanuts and winking and taking tricks.

I tried to tell the story no one had told me
or turned the pages for, but was telling itself
all by itself if you just looked and listened
and could sit still and remember what was before.

And then my mouth went shut. And Jessamine
led me up the stairs and put me to bed
and touched my lips in the dark with one dark finger,
saying, *Hush, hush,* but I'd hushed myself already.

The Other House

As a boy, I haunted an abandoned house
whose basement was always full of dark-green water
or dark-green ice in winter,
where frogs came back to life and sang each spring.

On broken concrete under the skeleton
of a roof, inside ribbed walls, I listened alone
where the basement stairs went down
under the water, down into that music.

During storms, our proper house would be flooded too.
The water would spout from drains, through the foundation
and climb the basement stairs
but silently, and would go away silently,

as silent as my father and mother were
all day and during dinner and after
and after the radio
without a murmur all the way into sleep.

All winter, the frogs slept in an icy bed,
remembering how to sing when it melted.
If I made a sound, they stopped
and listened to me sing nothing, singing nothing.

But gradually, finally April would come pouring
out of their green throats in a green chorus
to chorus me home toward silence.
Theirs was the only house that sang all night.

My Snake

By the railroad tracks, on cinders,
at the feet of brown cattails,
I found a snake stretched out in curves on its back.

Its belly was the color of clear water,
a green I could see through
to a place on fire.

The cross-hatched bruises near the tail
and the broken head meant a boy like me
had killed it. That was how

everyone I knew
told snakes to go away. I don't know why
I ran home then, found an empty jar, and ran

all the way back to it,
but for the first time in eight years,
I held a snake in the air with my own fingers.

It was almost as tall as I was and beautiful.
It swayed with me, then coiled
tail-first down into that mouth

and around the inside of the glass as evenly
and easily as if it was meant to be there
all along. I wanted to keep it

from more harm and from grown-up men
who killed them too. I wanted it to be mine
and still alive. I carried it home slowly

to a shelf on our back porch
where no one could quite see it
unless they looked on purpose. It sat there

coiled tight around itself and melting
for three whole days. For three nights
it coiled and melted in my dreams and half sleep.

I walked to school and came back. I ate my food.
I felt afraid. I couldn't look at it again.
I slept. I dreamed

I shivered out of bed
barefoot, carried the jar along our alley
in the night through patches of sandburs,

and poured the limp, uncoiling body
and all its rusty matter
into the rustier water of the swamp.

Maybe I really did. It was gone in the morning.
Or maybe my mother did it or my father.
None of us ever said a word about it.

The Fan Dance

I was seven and Sally Rand wasn't wearing
    anything. She was up there
        dancing with two quivery pink fans
like ostrich wings, and she was holding one
    around in back of her and the other
        in front of some of her, but was taking turns
switching them back and forth as she peeked out
    like a bird who'd lost her feathers but had found some
        others and wasn't quite sure where
or how to put them on—did they belong here
    or there?—but they wouldn't stay there
        or here while she was turning in slow circles
to violins, and if you were quick, you could see
    through the rosy light something
        like one breast from halfway
behind and half a rose-pink behind before
    another side of another breast
        and the other half behind had come around
to disappear at the rosier pink ends
    of feathers. And then she was gone
        offstage, and my small mother was leading me
and my big rosy-faced father up the aisle
    and out together onto the Midway
        of the Century of Progress and saying,
I don't think David should have seen that,
    and my father with his head down saying, *It* was
        rather suggestive, and I, who hadn't suggested
anything, ate Jack Armstrong candy
    in the back seat, with my Buck Rogers Ray Gun
        going *Zap!* and *Zap! Zap! Zap!* all the way home.

Whistler's Mother

My father said his mother bought it for him.
In each of the seven houses where I grew up
she hung in a hallway. She was sitting sideways,
looking like she'd been told to please get ready
to have her picture painted on Sunday
and had put on Sunday clothes as colorless
as the wallpaper and been told she should sit
still, and she wasn't used to being told.

She looked like she had pork and sauerkraut
in the oven and could smell it starting to burn.
She looked like she was listening for the doorbell
or the telephone to ring any minute now.
She looked like she didn't feel very much like being
anybody's mother today, thank you.
It was the only art my father owned.

The Red Hat

The lady had come right through the front door
to visit Grandma without being asked in.
They sat in the living room and talked and talked
about false neighbors and how sad it was
that nobody told the truth to anybody.

In the next room, I sank deep in my chair,
trying to read the Bible which would be good
for learning how to think and my education
and growing up and being morally upright
and better than comic books and private eyes.

Gradually Grandma had fallen silent.
The lady was telling her about bad things
years ago that were happening again.
Then slowly she backed out onto the porch
and let in flies and scurried away still talking.

Grandma touched my hand. She apologized.
She said the lady was old and had turned older
sooner than her friends and felt afraid
they'd forgotten who she was and were making up
bad stories about her and telling them to each other.

They thought she wasn't all there, though she was, she was.
They were all false witnesses and Pharisees.
A half hour later, in Deuteronomy 20,
I found false witnesses paid eyes for eyes
and teeth for teeth back then. I went to ask Grandma

why, but she only said, "She forgot her hat"
and held up a red felt thing with a red feather
and a black veil, like a bird caught in a net.
"Take it to her," she said, "or she'll come back.
Her house is right over there," she said and pointed.

This is too long a story. Here in the middle
I'm worried I'm telling it like an old lady
or an old man who can't remember exactly
what to say or which part to explain,
who should spend a lot more time just keeping quiet.

So here's the rest in a hurry. I went to the house
I thought Grandma had pointed at. I knocked
on the screen door. When nobody answered,
I opened it, threw the hat inside, and ran.
Almost a block away, Grandma was yelling,

"Wrong house!" I went back. An angry black man
came out of the door and threw the hat at me
like something dirty. I grabbed it and trespassed
through his garden to next door. The lady was standing
smiling behind her screen with her clothes off.

The First Touch

You sat in the two-seat wooden swing in the park
under the latticework of the moonlight
side by side with Sarah Downey your lips
a part of hers your good right arm gone numb
around her shoulders your good left hand at its first
touch of a breast becoming no longer hers
but yours in the heady distillates of the night
suspended in misty air by Lever Brothers
and the Union Carbide and Carbon Company
around you in and out of every breath
you took from each other you had only one
close encounter like this you lived too far
apart the storage tanks and the cat-crackers
of the largest oil refinery in the world
were fenced and barbed between you two forever
beyond the reach of your arms and bicycles.

Elegy for a Safety Man

In memoriam Richard Bell (1925–45)

He was our safety man, our last defense,
but off the field, he didn't believe in safety.

He was the first to sleep all night with a girl
and get caught, the only one who could stand

on the edge of a building roof at night in the wind,
who could siphon gasoline and not throw up.

He could drink a 12-ounce Pepsi in eight seconds,
the time it took to pour one out on the ground.

At the swimming pool, he'd stay under water so long,
we'd panic before he did and haul him out.

We had to hold him back one night when, drunk
on a single beer, he tried to tackle a car.

He was lanky and raw-boned and curly-haired
and smiled about as often as Gary Cooper.

He didn't worship heroes or act like one.
He didn't quite flunk any subject in school.

He joined the Marines, was shipped to the South Pacific
where no one close could be afraid for him.

He jogged with a tank across a broken field
and was the first of us to disappear.

How Johnny Nolan Rescued Me

The swimming instructor told us,
You're on fire. Your ship is sinking
at night and spilling oil.
You're overboard. A shipmate
is floundering near you, choking.
He can't swim, and he's forgotten
how to do anything
but wave his arms and holler.

Fifty of us stood there
naked along the edge
of the pool. He paired us off,
and I faced Johnny Nolan,
who, for a change, followed
instructions, dove and swam
through ordinary seamen,
then screamed at me, treading water.

He was six feet three, an All-
American tackle. I'd seen him
extract a louder, drunker
fraternity man (who had laughed
at his skin-tight "sailor suit")
out of a sports car window
offhandedly, hold him up
high under a streetlight,

and listen to his confession
before putting him back
feet first. I swam toward him
slowly. Twenty-four actors

enjoyed themselves nearby,
squealing and shrieking, pretending
to sputter and gag, and Johnny,
who could have drowned

all forty-nine of us
and the instructor, held still
as I drifted closer. He smiled.
He became lighter than water.
He became lighter than air.
He let me guide him back,
afloat through the quality
of mercy to the gutter.

Passing the Road Gang

I could see them ahead of us,
fifty or more of them
doing hard time, strung along
one bank of an Ozark road,
stripped to the waist, shoveling
fill dirt and whacking weeds,
with two guards in the shade
of a shagbark hickory
and two more with shotguns
at each end of the line.

I had nowhere to turn,
nowhere to get away
or hide. I was being driven
by freckle-faced blonde Diane
whose sunsuit left no more
and no less to the imagi-
nation than the sun
on her topless convertible.

I shrank into myself
as one by one we passed
those prisoners who straightened,
swiveled their heads, and stared
after us, giving up
a series of wild laments
with staccato diminuendos
to punish God and themselves
and me as we dwindled away
to our separate vanishing points.

Curtsy

My daughters are to perform
for the first time in public
    in costumes all the way
    to the floor. They show me
how they can curtsy
in the kitchen. With forefingers
    and thumb tips, we suspend
    a make-believe skirt, swivel
our right sneaker behind
our left, dip our knee,
    then stand up straight again
    and simper. They want me to try,
and as I sink and wobble,
my back nearly as straight
    as it ever was, I tell them
    gentlemen are supposed to
bend at the hips stiffly
or duck their heads quickly
    or do both simultaneously,
    and the curious word *curtsy*
used to mean *courtesy*
which before that had to do
    with what you did in a court,
    not for a judge but a king
and a queen, and they say, *Daddy,*
never mind all that.

Talk

It's her turn to stand up there all alone
in front of the blackboard and be an explorer,
in her case, Admiral Peary telling about
trying to find the Pole in a fur hat
and beard, with a stick pointing at a map
showing exactly wherever whatever happened
beginning to end and why, remembering
to make eye contact (she does), not shifting around
or shuffling (she doesn't) but being poised, remaining
comfortable unless she has a reason
for moving along with a few well-chosen words
to explain what was (or wasn't quite) discovered
(she does), not spending valuable time explaining
what people already know (she doesn't) and willing
to answer questions (she is) if she knows the answers
(and she does), then going directly to her seat
(she goes there) with as much of a straight face
behind her beard as her most attentive student
can see from the visitor's row, while promising
himself to follow her very good example.

Crane Fly

The first crane fly of spring
is in the bathtub. My girls,
like maids in an operetta
emoting over a mouse,
are all atwitter. They want me
to kill it. They hand me
the daily news for a swatter
and are hovering nearby,
afraid to look, but looking.

I've told them every year
the crane flies come flying
out of the grass in zigzags,
looking for mates and places
to lay eggs and get confused
and blunder into houses.

I've shown them insect guides,
but anything airborne
that isn't a moth or a fly
is a bee and ready to sting.
It's a kind of daddy longlegs,
I say, but they don't like them
either. So I give up,
and having no butterfly net
or handy window to help
this awkward, fragile creature
out of the house to live
and die some other day,
I give it a swat and gather
the wings and the ochre thorax,
the thread-thin, disjointed legs,

which weren't meant to last
very long (I tell myself),
in a piece of tissue. The girls
thank me, their voices subdued,
their faces as serious,
looking at me, as mine.

Homework in Social Studies

My daughters watch the polite young service man,
who had been under our car changing our oil,
who'd given them both suckers and called them cute,
being arrested by sheriff's deputies
outside the garage, handcuffed and patted down,
having his jeans yanked past his boxer shorts
for further investigation, and taken away
because, as his partner says, of "an old warrant."

I drive us all toward home down the same road.
They want to know what an old warrant is—
some kind of crime? I mumble a slightly more
paralegal answer: a piece of paper
signed by a judge that tells the policemen
to arrest somebody, in this case maybe because
he'd broken a law and had to answer questions
standing up in a county court and hadn't.

I tried to explain how judges could tell sheriffs
they had to do something or could give them the right
to do it their own way. The girls are listening
suspiciously, as if I might be a teacher
telling them something they could be graded on.

They'd liked that nice young man. The sucker sticks
are still there in the corners of their mouths.
They're looking through the windshield cautiously
at a world coming at them, passing on both sides,
just under the limit.

Castle

She forgot. She has to make one for her class
    by tomorrow. It has to have two gates
        and a workable drawbridge
and crenellated towers and walls with embrasures
    and a castle keep. It has to have a stable
        and a murder hole and a moat
and fit on a card table. She has a bag
    of toilet-paper rolls, strips of foam-plastic,
        a pad of construction paper, tacky glue,
a clutch of Popsicle sticks, and a frantic
    eleventh-hour assistant. After hours
        of labor and sleep and a double-quick
spray painting which covers almost all
    the clauses of elementary building codes,
        her assistant sees their project tilting and scraping
through a classroom door, and later on that day,
    it passes with flying pennons. Yet in half-sleep,
        obedient to some robber baron
in his head, he goes on gluing cardboard dunce-caps
    on castle towers and hoisting gates with watch-chains
        through screw-eyes, though he doesn't believe
in fixed redoubts where all the insiders play
    and fatten on fair game till they're wiped out
        by what they used to think were inferior
masterless men who then take turns being killed
    and replaced by tourists. He burrows deeper
        into sleep like a fox or a badger,
like a hedgehog, like a mole, like a worm
    who make their castles out of earth
        on earth, with more ways in and down and out.

My Father's Dance

He thought of his body sometimes, when he had to,
as something to go to work with, then bring back,
wash off, cover up, and forget about as soon
as possible till it went on the next shift.

At home he played old songs on the piano
and sang them, swaying on the bench to "Nola"
and "Piccolo Pete" and hitting the lowest notes
of "The Bells in the Lighthouse" and "Asleep in the Deep."

After years of working at it, he gave up
wanting to be invisible in public,
but still didn't like being noticed. He'd sit in the back
or, better yet, would stand in the back near the door

just in case. But that was only in halls
where the lights stayed on. If it was going to be dark,
he'd usher us and his body down the aisle
to the best seats he could find up near the stage

and forget himself. I'd watch his face come alive
and the light of joy go dancing across his glasses
as hoofers like Ebsen, Bolger, or Bojangles
carried him away on the tips of their toes.

In all his eighty-odd years, he never once
would take a first shy step on a dance floor
(which is any floor anywhere or broken concrete
or dirt or water or air if you trust the music),

But now he's going to. Here, in my lifetime,
I'm nearly in sole charge of his memory
and the heavy ghost of his body. I'm leading it
out onto this floor and saying, *Dance.*

2

The Invitation

I loaf and invite my soul. Walt Whitman
    began a poem that way. It was probably how
        (without those words) he began most of his poems.
He disengaged himself from the whole welter
    of obligations, from what he *should* be doing
        in his other world, and *invited*
(the politest word of all) a guest
    to visit him, bad timing and temperaments
        and whims and more impersonal intrusions
permitting. It implied the expectation
    of pleasing and being pleased, of honoring
        and being honored by good company.
Yet Whitman doesn't say how often the soul
    had declined the invitation without regrets
        or even a word, how often it had sent
a momentarily plausible imposter
    in its place to turn their meeting to bickering,
        tedious quarreling, interrupted only
by silences. He doesn't list the occasions
    when his soul had invited *him* and had swept him
        off his feet to a different party—a trial
by fire or a public execution of comrades
    or a mandatory dance where he was left
        helpless to keep his balance, no loafer now,
but a disengaged uncritical witness
    to the meaning of *naked power,* who discovered,
        between the ends of his first two fingers and thumb,
blades of green grass which were withering
    before he could guess what they were
        or dream up any metaphors to describe them.

What Do I Know?

That was the question he kept asking
before he began writing. Montaigne
    in his leisurely wisdom would answer
    with an essay of understanding
himself among others. Often
at the end of one more day of trying
    to answer even more obvious questions
    of my own, I seem to know
less than I did to start with,
which was little enough. Suppose I take
    for a hard example, How to Write
    a Poem. I don't, of course, know Why,
though Where and When and To What
Extent seem comprehensible
    once in a while. Did Montaigne mean
    What do I dare put down in words
that someone else might possibly read
with pleasure or profit or even some useful
    exasperation? Because I almost
    never know anything but a roster
of cold cold facts, I'm obliged to hope
my record of puzzlement may be
    enough. At the end of a poem, poets
    often allow themselves to imply
they understand whatever it was
they thought they were writing about. They may send
    backwards a shower of appreciation
    over their own misunderstanding
from which they are now blessedly
delivered and have given over
    to the known and knowing world. They may drop
    the last brick at the top of the heap

they hope is a pyramid. They may click
shut the lid of the box or finally touch
    with the snake's tongue the strange tip
    of its own tail, not knowing what it is.

A Lesson from a Student

My student says he writes short stories and poems
in front of a mirror, sitting at a table
in the nude. He says he feels more inspired
when he sees himself at work with nothing to hide,
with nothing to be ashamed of or afraid of.
Although this young man's poems come to a stop
almost before they begin, and his short stories
go on and on till they almost meet themselves
coming back, instead of telling him
it's the worst idea I've heard in a long while,
I try it myself.
         And there I am in the mirror
in the bleak interrogation room again
in the small hours, having been shaken awake,
frog-marched, and stripped. There, on the other side
of the glass, behind that translucent image
of what's to become of me, the official,
who already knows the answers to all the questions
I've kept to myself, is staring through me now
as if I'm neither here nor there. The papers lying
in front of me are filled with my scrawled confession,
which, instead of stopping cold, goes on and on.

An Assignment for Student Playwrights

I told them to go listen to people talking,
to write exactly how some people really
talked to each other, and one young man
came to the next workshop, looking bewildered,
holding his notes by thumb tip and fingertip
to avoid contamination. He said, "This
is how they talked. They weren't actually
having a conversation, just interrupting
each other saying whatever it was
they wanted to keep on saying. They had to decide
today, here and now, like whether to go on
with this, this whatever-it-was they couldn't
think of a name for. They kept looking
this way or that way, even at me (I wasn't
anybody, just some student scribbling),
but never at each other. You could tell
they felt bad. They were making up their minds
about something important enough to change
their lives maybe forever. But what was coming
out of their mouths wouldn't have passed even
middle-school English. They were both trying to say
what hurt, what was disappointing, what wasn't
even common courtesy, let alone love.
If they'd been actors, good ones, they'd have been making
contact. They'd have been improvising something
more interesting than shoving their chairs back
and standing up and trying to split the bill
but dividing it wrong, dropping it, picking it up,
and arguing all the way out. Now what the hell
am I supposed to make out of this crap?"

In the Green Room

She's sitting there between acts
She's knitting and purling
    while glancing at dog-eared sides
    of an old romance. Last week
she was reading about crocheting
and *Lady Chatterley,*
    absorbing both. She gathers
    the ruffled, rumpled, wrinkled
pleats of her skirt together
in her lap and fans at her legs.
    She hardly has to be
    anyone as she murmurs
by heart (without once looking)
to her lord, her incompetent lover,
    and her interesting murderer,
    and skims an article
on how to revive a marriage
on the rocks. She hears her cue.
    Her legs regather and lengthen.
    Her skirt falls into place
for a change of scene. Her hands
are empty now. Her face
    is full of a self she follows
    into a dazzling light.

The Heaven of Actors

At rise, the house lights darken.
The overhead lights and the lights
in the wings and the footlights
go on, and our gray actors
shine again, no longer
merely themselves, but the many
they were always meant to be,
their bodies, faces, and voices
turning and changing again
like young heavenly objects
endlessly reembodied,
their wardrobes as various
as the wonders of new stars
perpetually recast
on their revolving stages
on all their opening nights.

A Visitor Calls on Joseph Conrad

He was shown the way to wait in the library
    because the master of that country house
        was writing and could not suffer
interruption now. The visitor
    lost count of the books spilling from bookshelves
        or disarranged on the floor of the dim room.
They seemed to be interrupting or contradicting
    their separate languages, their premises,
        and each other's most unseaworthy calculations
except for one corner where the visitor found,
    neatly, compactly, and securely ranked,
        the atlases and star-charts, the manuals
for damage control, for fire and steam and storm,
    for seamanship and for abandoning ship,
        for all the rules of the road. What light there was
came through French doors. Beyond them, he could see
    a small, neglected courtyard and shut doors
        which now sprang open as a frock-coated man
came stumbling out, his ragged mustache and beard
    parting around the snags of his crooked teeth
        in a snarl of despair. Two sheets of manuscript
were fluttering down behind him. He flung himself
    face down into the weeds and began pounding
        his half-clenched fists on the ground, kicking it,
kicking it with the toes of his polished shoes.
    The same quiet, upright, strait-laced woman
        who had shown the visitor so calmly and firmly
where he should wait came out into daylight,
    stepped carefully down, bent down and lifted the man
        calmly and firmly upright, steadied him,
collected the dropped pages calmly and placed them
    firmly into his small hands, then steered him
        implacably up and back into darkness.

Catfish

A memory of Richard Hugo

We'd caught all five of them that afternoon,
had brought them to his house still sluggish, writhing
in a pail of water dipped from their own bed.
It was as dark as they were and shallower.
They couldn't move except around each other.

We talked about poetry and our own poems.
I sat in a Goodwill chair, and he presided
at the kitchen sink, lined it with newspapers,
lifted one fish behind its squirming barbels
and laid it belly up on the evening news.

We agreed some critics misunderstood the ear
and the wild inventive iambic pentameter
of Wyatt and Donne, mistook their subtle voices
for clumsiness. One catfish lost its head
in a fist that held it down like an example

of something tougher than hell to come to terms with,
and a pair of pliers began peeling the skin
inside out like a sleeve or a turtleneck
away from flesh, tugged it down and around,
jerking it loose while the other fist held on.

We couldn't think of a single formula
to keep the living and breathing human voice
alive above a mechanical ground beat
unless an instrumentally inspired
jazz soloist was playing against strict time.

When all five gutted catfish lay in a row,
raw, on paper, rinsed, then neatly foiled,
dated, stacked, to be frozen and someday thawed,
sniffed at, remembered, eaten or thrown away,
we walked to the nearest tavern and drank dinner.

Mr. Bones

A footnote for John Berryman's
Dream Songs

Ranchers and townspeople and sodbusters
called them that whenever they saw their wagons—
high-sided, dead slow—-in spring all heading out
onto the empty prairie in no hurry.
What they were after wouldn't run away.

And there was plenty of it for everybody,
armloads at a time from the slumped, half-scattered,
sun-bleached heaps in the grass near water holes
or farther apart on trails those very bones
had made long ago when they were still together.

Each Mr. Bones, for years on end, would carry
his share of load after load to the freight scales
at the nearest station and ship them all back East
to be ground to dust and put to ground again
in public and private gardens among flowers.

On Being Asked by an Assistant to
the Governor of the State of Washington
for an Appropriate Quotation
from a Native American to Conclude
an Inaugural Speech

I said what Leschi said on the gallows
where another governor had sent him to die
on the evidence of lying city fathers
before they engraved his name on a picnic beach.

I said what Chief Sealth said when he saw
the Moving People take his people's place
and name it after him. To save the expense
of spirits like them I said I had nothing to say.

An Assignment for Senior Citizens

Our teachers are mostly dead now, the easy marks,
the mothers, the gorgons, and the honest clowns,
the amateur magicians, the anxious wizards
of osmosis, and the genuine articles.

Let's think of those whose faces we still remember.
Some didn't give enough credit to what we thought
we were, but most had hopes we'd finally do,
almost any day now, what we were born for.

Again and again some told us we'd be sorry
we hadn't listened to what they tried to teach
in their searching, questioning, celebrating voices—
everything we couldn't have taught ourselves.

We and our fellow sufferers, brownnosers, friends,
the upper upper-classmates, the dropouts
still alive and even the dead ones
should finish all our homework and turn it in.

Trying to Write a Poem
While the Couple in the Apartment Overhead
Make Love

She's like a singer straying slowly off key
    while trying too hard to remember the words to a song
        without words, and her accompanist
is metronomically dead set
    to sustain her pitch and tempo, and meanwhile,
        under their feathers and springs, under their carpet,
under my own ceiling, I try to go on
    making something or other out of nothing
        but those missing words, whose rhythm is only
predictable for unpredictable moments
    and then erratic, unforeseeable even
        at its source where it ought to be abundantly,
even painfully clear. A song is a series of vowels
    interrupted and shaped by consonants
        and silence, and gifted singers say if you can
pronounce words and remember how to breathe,
    you can sing. Although I know some words by heart
        and think I know how to breathe (even down here
at work alone) and may be able sometimes
    to write some of them down, right now it seems
        improbable they'll have anything much like
the permissive diction, the mounting cadences,
    now, or then, or now again the suspended
        poise, the drift backward, the surprise
of the suddenly almost soundless catch
    of the caught breath, the quick
        loss of support
which wasn't lost at all as it turns out
    but found again and even again
        somewhere, in midair, far, far above me.

The Moth

I was giving a poetry reading on a stage
and was nearly finished. Out of the darkness
of the audience, a white moth fluttered
into the light. It clung to the back of my hand.
I felt afraid for it. I lost my place.
I forgot I was supposed to be saying something.
I felt I didn't need to say anything.
I carried it carefully into the empty wings
and out of the stage door into the night
and let it fly away at the end of a dream.

3

In Youngs Creek

All three of us stood still
among tall fir trees. Two
had been wading slowly downstream
in silence but for the rush
of shallow water. The third
had been crossing from bank to bank
but had paused, one foreleg
lifted, one small black hoof
glistening in the sun.

None of us moved. Our eyes
looked out into other eyes,
trying to understand
what we were and where
all three were going to be
in a moment, from that moment
on and whether to trust
what was holding us together,
whether to let the clear, cold
rippling water around us
be the one and only language.

Two of us, years later,
still stand there, still deciding
whether to move or whisper,
while the third makes up its mind
to trust creatures so strange,
so near, then turns away
as deliberately and slowly
as before, crosses the streams
of water and light onto stones,
onto moss, and disappears.

Stopping along the Way

Heading south toward campus, my car
    stops suddenly, abruptly, almost
on its own. My right foot
    has found the brake pedal
before my eyes can admire
    a very young possum strolling
across our right of way
    at his personal intersection
of human cross-purposes,
    some of whose brakes are squeaking
behind us now. The possum
    pauses, lowers his gray-pink-
and-sooty snout to drink in
    the odor of something
among the fallen and flattened
    sycamore leaves. I've seen
too many of him lying down
    even flatter than seemed
possible beside roads
    and in gutters. I realize
my car's mere presence looming
    over him won't quicken
those four deliberate paws,
    won't urge him out of danger,
but before I can think or make
    some warning sign, two cars
are honking. He lifts his head
    dreamily, comparing
that sound to some distant sound
    somewhere deep, far back
in his old, new mind, then begins
    strolling forward again

and up onto the grass
    among the unloaded, locked,
and abandoned bicycles
    and empties and leaflets left
by fraternal and sisterly
    orders on their own ways
to and from understanding
    or back to forbidden gardens
and holes in the ground. Again
    a car behind me honks.
And another. It's what geese do
    heading south at the beginning
of winter. They want to know
    the one in front still believes
they're there and are trusting him
    to be sure where they're all going.

Blind Instinct

I didn't call it that
    on my knees in the gutter
after a hard rain,
    watching an earthworm
upstream of a sewer grid
    trying to save itself
by straining frantically,
    corkscrewing its body
the only ways it knew
    as a born non-swimmer
without fins, without eyes to squeeze
    shut, without an instructor
in water that wouldn't stay
    where it was supposed to be.
In another school, our teacher
    showed us what worms know:
they can tell up from down,
    can turn away from too cold,
too hot, too salty, too much,
    too soon, too far away.
They know it from end to end
    inside that string of hearts
we found by slicing one
    open. It slid
(before I could hold it here)
    over the edge and was gone
back out to sea again.

That Bird

That bird can see your feet walking in the wrong direction.
It can see your clumsy hands bringing something useless
toward your mouth. When water touches the sand and draws away
and touches the sand again and draws away, that bird
knows where you should stand and where you should look
and whether your hands should be open, should hold each other,
or be shut. That bird asks nothing more from you than a place
to make its nest behind your shoulders, against your spine.

Meadowlark

You may be walking on the edge of a road,
humming a song from the hit parade of your youth
when you believed what you sang, when everything
you believed in had to be some kind of singing.

A bird may surprise you then with a song somewhere
above or behind you, maybe just ahead—
the three directions you'd almost given up on,
places you thought might have no songs at all.

If you stop to find the source, maybe you'll see
a yellow-and-black-bibbed singer perched on a post
or on barbed wire, staking his claim on a muddle
of worthless weeds and grass by uttering,

as if with two tongues, his plaintive minor duet
from two of his throats, one of them nearly yours,
now bursting open like a pair of wildflowers
under the sun, even as you stand there.

A Pastoral Elegy for a Pasture

Pause here at the edge of a field
beside the newly sprouted offspring
    of the grass that brought us all to life
    and has kept returning
year after year despite all herdsmen
and horsemen and lately the small flock
    of an old bachelor shepherd
    whose sheep are gone. The devastated lambs
and ewes and the de-horned rams
with their full scrotums have gone
    where sheep have always gone. Our natures,
    in the forms of two surveyors,
their transit, a bulldozer, and an earth-mover,
are turning aside what was left
    of a spring pasture. They heap it now
    around four-square foundations
of houses-to-be, which are his memorial
along with these few words
    made of morning air,
    which will contain no anguish,
no shower of tears
falling out of the sky, no refrain,
    no diatribe against the responsible
    irresponsible gods,
no mournful noise,
but a brief silence.

Watching a Boa Constrictor Yawn

it held its breath somewhere down there in a coil
inside a muscular wilderness beyond
a velvety gray-pink mouth whose convolutions
were folded almost shut on a forked tongue,
but now, its jawbone nearly unhinged, it sighs
and slowly brings together what could have swallowed
an egg or a whole rat or a suckling pig
with Adam's old apple in its mouth. With nothing
better or worse to do, unable to blink
away what trembles in front of them, its eyes
content themselves with staring into mine.

The Escaped Gorilla

When he walked out in the park that early evening
just before closing time, he didn't take
the nearest blonde in one arm and climb a tree
to wait for the camera crews. He didn't savage
anyone in uniform, upend cars
or beat his chest or scream, and nobody screamed
when they found him hiding behind the holly hedge
by the zoo office where he waited for someone

to take him by the hand and walk with him
around two corners and along a pathway
through the one door that wasn't supposed to be open
and back to the oblong place with the hard sky
where all of his unbreakable toys were waiting
to be broken, with the wall he could see through,
but not as far as the place he almost remembered,
which was too far away to be anywhere.

Judging a Hog

Adapted from The Elements of Livestock Judging,
W. W. Smith, 1927

He must be observed from both sides and the front
and from above while you are standing close
at a rear view. The common defects: light hams,
pinched loins, rough shoulders, and knock knees.

You determine the depth of fat with your firm palm
pressed up or down or in. The hair should be fine
and straight, lying flat. The head should be light
and the skin soft, no tendency to wrinkling.

His ears are never silk purses. Above the neck
is all cheap meat and waste, the smaller the better.
All parts are salable, but a broad, chunky,
strongly arched back, smooth, regular, deep sides,

and a trim, straight underline are the most
desirable—chest full, forequarters squared,
legs wide apart. The worst: a heavy paunch,
a waisty belly curve, and a fish back.

You will find some hogs impatient with your judging.
Some will show signs of indifference to breeding.
Some will exhibit uncharacteristic feelings
of assertiveness and a disregard for the orders

of their owners, rings in their noses notwithstanding.
Remember you have ribbons at your disposal
and the power to redeem sinners. Don't be misled
by a pink two-hole snout slippery with mucus

and speckled with sawdust. It is irrelevant
in all your judgments. In spite of what you may feel
surging against you sideways or lunging forward
at the end of a leash, the toss of a thick skull

or the heft and fortitude of testicles
the size of udders, you make careful notes.

Thoreau and the Mud Turtle

The muddy nest was empty except for one
    inch-and-a-half-long hatchling at the edge,
        motionless. He knelt beside it,
wondering what was wrong. There was no trace
    of the others. They'd either made the dry,
        dangerous journey to the brook
or had been caught by crows, raccoons, or otters.
    He lifted this runt of the litter
        from among the broken shells and watched it
crawl one foot per minute. Whenever he moved
    even an inch, it froze,
        pulled in its beak and legs, and waited.
He waited too till its green head came out
    and looked, listened, then wrongheadedly
        chose a longer way. He scolded it,
picked it up, and went marching to the shore,
    but hesitated there, afraid
        he might be thwarting nature's merciless plan
that had left the weakest to die
    for the sake of stronger, smarter,
        and quicker turtles to come. So he set it down
and let it choose. It held still for a moment,
    then suddenly turned and scuttled into the current,
        tilted, swirled, and was spun away downstream.

The Elephant's Graveyard

Their huge gray shapes were trudging up a trail
    against the side of a cliff and around curves
        and up across the screen near the shaky end
of Tarzan's movie. They looked tired
    and old. They were going somewhere
        they didn't want to go but were going
together so they could finally lie down
    and be alone on the bare gray ground
        among stones, which were all the same shade
on the screen except for the skulls already
    empty, out in the open there, and the new tusks.
        We all agreed with Tarzan and Jane: the hunters
still down in the thick jungle going crazy
    should leave them alone. We agreed out loud
        in the front row and up in the balcony
only the old ones should go to the graveyard.
    The young ones should stay down there in the jungle,
        splashing in the river. Later that summer
the circus came to town. We joined the parade
    and watched real elephants wearing canvas rainbows
        over gray skin, some with women waving
from the backs of their necks. They shuffled along
    119th Street past our theater
        looking old and tired, even the middle-sized
who were holding on to the tails of the big ones.
    The two smallest, running to keep up,
        kept losing their grip, kept having to run faster,
to hold on with the very ends of their trunks,
    with one pink finger, to the end of the tail end
        of the one ahead who knew where it was going.

Falling Behind

Among migrating baboons, if a female
is sick or injured, she doesn't survive long.
An adult male will drop back sometimes
and walk beside her if she has a young one,
but she has to try too hard
to keep up with the rest. She has no time
to eat or to feed another,
so she lags farther and farther behind and grows weaker
and finally can't move.

She crouches or lies down then
to hide a part of herself and her child somewhere
low among grass, while the others,
traveling on the open plain together,
grow smaller and smaller.

The Hunters

Bibs said we were going hunting, and what Bibs said
we did that year before high school. I thought he must need me
(like when he would shoplift) to be his boy-scout lookout.

He led the way through our swamp among cattails
and sand hummocks at the edge of the lake
to a thicket of half-grown poplars, the only trees.

His slingshot was like mine—a forked stick
and a slice of inner-tube—and I didn't think
anyone could hit anything but tin cans,

not even Bibs. So when he crouched and held still
and waited, then shuffled sideways
and forward slowly and held a stone

drawn back and pinched in the angle, I crouched
like him, behind him, and followed his lead,
thinking this was a good game. When the dove

couldn't bear to have us so close to her nest
and coming closer, she burst out of the shadows
of leaves and hovered there, flapping and frantic,

and Bibs stood up and aimed and let the stone go,
and it flew before the dove could. I heard it
thud, then heard the other thud when she fell.

And Bibs was jumping and cheering, almost dancing,
and running toward her, both his arms in the air
and kneeling beside her. I leaned over his shoulder.

I watched her do her best not to die so close
to our strange faces. When she did,
Bibs slid his right hand under her, lifted her,

rubbed and admired the sheen of her breast feathers,
and then began to pluck them. He said his mother
would thank him for it and cook it for his father

who would eat it for dinner and give him the bones after,
the ones he couldn't crunch, to make something with
like they did in the old country. He hurried away,

cutting across the swamp through shallows and mud
and leaving a kind of trail I couldn't follow.
I sat in the reeds, then took the long way home.

For the Man Who Taught Tricks to Owls

You say they were slow to learn. The brains of owls
    went down in your opinion through long hours
        of unresponsive staring
while you showed them how to act out minor parts
    in the world of Harry Potter. Come with me now
        into the night, perch motionless, balanced
on a branch above a thicket, where every choice
    of a flight path is more narrow
        than your broad wingspan, more jagged
and crooked than patterns of interrupted moonlight
    on twigs and fallen leaves, where what you take
        in silence with claws and beak to stay alive
knows everything about you except your tricks,
    except where you're going to be in the next instant
        and how you got there without anyone's help.

On a Glass of Ale under a Reading Lamp

My fingers go around it
   and so do the small flies.
They too want something
   headier than night air
and lamplight. They don't know
   what they're after either
but have more than one sense
   of where it is,
and it grows more and more
   desirable as they give in
to their desire. Why else
   were they given wings? The right way
is here almost at the lips
   of this other thirsty creature
who is risking a desire
   like them to drink without drowning,
whose hand is hovering
   in the light to show them how
to touch good bitterness
   again, not knowing why.

4

Owning a Creek

A barn with a concrete floor, gutters and drains
   for washing away cow pies and spilled milk.
      Three stalls, their edges bitten
and splintered by generations
   of barn-sour horses. A matter-of-fact garden
      with a hoe still stuck in a furrow. A four-square
shotgun house with a roof and a welcome mat
   and shutters on all sides. An old orchard
      with eleven unpruned prune trees. All ten acres
available. You should buy it, the man said.
   Fix up the fences, paint everything white,
      call it a nice name on a sign out front,
and sell it to city folks as thoroughbred stables.
   A sure thing. I walked out back, alone,
      with the advice but not the consent of the crows,
and waded through knee-high crack grass (inedible
   by anything but fire) to the south boundary,
      the bank of a creek. Whoever bought the farm
would own on paper a good seventy yards
   of one side of this creek glittering now
      and always out of a forest, out of the foothills,
down from a mountain lake. For the first time
   I was tempted, but had just enough sense
      to kneel and put my hand against the stones
of its bed and leave it there in the cold current,
   in the rush swirling around it, past it, and gone,
      and all of me felt glad to be going with it.

Up against the Sea

At the foot of the cliff, the sea is taking back
what it left there long ago, and the landowners
have made a barricade of three old cars
between low and high tide and loaded them
with so many river stones, they've been weighed down
below their springs, below their shock absorbers.

The waves are breaking over the side panels,
on blurred teenage graffiti, and barnacles
and tougher limpets have made themselves at home
on mats and cushions, on the salt versions
of vinyl and rust. The sea is welcoming
all of them, as ever, as passengers
at the end of a lover's leap, at the beginning
of a joy ride down an old lover's lane again.

The Right Way

Epictetus said a man should approach death
with the calm of a traveler at a crossroads
asking a stranger which way he should turn
or whether to go straight on. He said we don't care
which is the right way as long as it's right.

But aren't some guides stranger? Don't some prefer
misguiding the half lost into shortcuts
or dangerous weather where a traveler
comes to a dead end and has to turn back
to the other death he'd wanted to leave behind?

On an Island

Whichever way you walk this beach,
you find on the one hand the sea
and on the other a dense interior
where you recall clawing
through thickets and snags of vines, believing
> you had lost yourself
> in an underworld where anything
> might happen, where you might yet discover
> what only the trees had understood,
> a place where your feet would stay
beside each other, where your bare hands
would touch something
beyond their emptiness. But stumbling
finally out into the open,
you found only that same flat sea
> again ahead of you, that straight horizon
> which is beside you now and behind you
> here at this landmark.   You've come, as far
> as you can recall, exactly to where you were:
> to a stone at the edge of the surf
where you began, where now you end
once more a journey around
an isolated plot, where you pause
and reconsider the unromantic agony
of change without progress. Whichever way
> you walk, you find yourself
> beginning where you were and seeing
> what you tried your best to remember
> or dismiss and forget. But barnacles,
> mussels, and chitons are all here

setting a hard example, holding hard
against the rise and fall, the rush
and ebbing away of whatever
made them and put them here to live
and die among water, stone, and deadly air.

Rescue

You climbed alone, thinking
you were taking your mind
and your body (far more
    seriously than ever)
    up to some new level, all
    the way to the summit where
only a shaken few
had stood or knelt, dizzy
with joy. But they weren't ready
    to be there. You're at the end
    of a rope, on the brink,
    at a not quite utterly
deadly end stop, helpless,
hoping for help, and here
the rescuers come, slowly
    and more surely than you did,
    their eyes alert for fractures
    and measuring odd angles
of living rock, toe-holds
and hand-holds. They're comparing
your predicament with theirs,
    not one, not one of them
    is about to die
    for you. Their primary rule
is their own lives first. You may hear
shouting from somewhere
far away, may see them
    waving hello or goodbye
    which from point of view
    will seem the same
next spring if they come back,
lean over the edge, and wonder
where in the world you've gone.

Upstream

The river has almost nothing against you
but itself. Whatever you think you have in mind
is the opposite of this current, this moment
of turbulent, cold snowmelt from the mountains.
It's tumbling down through everything you supposed
was the only way to go where you were meant to.

Why be surprised to find what's left of your body
out of the mainstream, half ashore and still
half catching your breath in the cold shallows,
now lying crossways, one half staring at stones,
the other turned toward the sun?

Letting the Grass Grow under Your Feet

It would rather not
but of course it will.
If you've been standing on it
long enough, those blades
    will insist there's a way out
    from under and up at last
    into the light. You don't have to
    let it do that
because it *will.* No matter how
stubbornly or heavily you bear down,
something inside its cells
doesn't believe in you
    and your listless energy,
    your postponements
    of going somewhere else,
    of deciding where in the world
you belong. It will grow
sideways and turn yellow or under pressure
nearly white. It will turn
to an almost uprooted root
    for a while, then send those blades
    (in spite of how long
    you stand there in the way)
    out, up, and around you.

Cemetery Grass

The blades keep coming back.
They keep showing up
in the best possible light.

They rise together
but not quite long enough
to bear more seeds

or high enough to bend
and sway in the wind
under the summer sun

or out of it under the moon
like an old unruly crowd
of ghosts disturbing the night.

The man in the machine
is cutting them off short
among the remains of flowers.

The Heart of the Forest

You pretend to look for wildflowers, but what you're doing
is trying to find traces of where your feet
lost their sense of direction in the woods.

You can name the trees and what's staying alive
under them, but you're afraid this may be a time
when you find the ghost-pale, skinned corpses of beavers

or the green antlers still on the skulls of elk,
or the leaflike, feather-light wings of owls suspended
upside down on spikes among living branches,

so you rehearse remembering the place
where one of your clumsy feet once found itself
secure, where it lifted you and moved you,

where you breathed again and saw, in the near-darkness
of the forest floor, a fir tree fallen and broken
into nurse logs, out of whose rotten, moss-covered sides,

among small spillways of lilies of the valley,
dozens of other selves were growing, rooted
all the way through into another forest

where nothing comes to an end, where nothing is lost,
and lying down with one ear to the ground,
you listened to its heart and yours still beating.

5

Free Fall

At first he's making better and better time
in his descent toward an unavoidable
necessarily inevitable
conclusion against a remarkable-looking surface
no longer keeping its distance or its place
in the scheme of things and then the worldly limit
of acceleration thirty-two feet per second
per second in free fall will slow his body
down to a rough four hundred while he enjoys
the interval to notice the steadily
increasing size of the earth the inexorable
enlargement of its horizon the revelation
of all its topographical details
its clarifying and intensifying colors
and shades of meaning if he were a mouse
or any smaller creature and had the luck
to land where he wouldn't immediately be drowned
impaled or run over he'd go bouncing away
as good as new but as a heavyweight
contender and thinker he comes down now
to earth with entirely too much emphasis.

The Presumption of Death

If you've disappeared, if your body is no longer
    being seen in its customary places,
        has left no change of address,
has filled out no new forms for the forwarding
    of legal or personal questions or information,
        it is assumed to be, under the law
after seven years, no longer lighter than water
    or capable of moving by itself
        from one place to another
or likely to reappear in a meaningful pose
    among the comforts of home. Officially
        it will be no one. (Its status is not to be
confused with Civil Death, which is reserved
    for bodies in institutions trying their best
        to correct their poor behavior.) Wherever it is
at that particular time, no matter what
    you may be thinking of doing with it or for it
        or even inside it, the law will pronounce it dead.

For an Old Woman at the Gate

Your permission slip has been stapled, decoded, stamped,
   and handed over to the authorities,
      some of whom scan you now
and ask you to spread your arms, expecting you
   to fly all by yourself. One wants to see the insides
      of your shoes, your good shoes
as if you'd been complaining. Then he tries
   to ruin the heels. One snatches your purse and stands there
      rummaging through it, right in front of you,
thinking you won't remember what he looks like.
   He takes your book away and shakes it
      upside down, losing your place again.
He wants to know if you've been given a gift
   by a stranger, which was so long ago,
      it's none of his business now, not even yours.
People are watching you, being kept back
   from the scene of this accident, worried, afraid
      they might be forced to testify. Your belongings
have all been carried off somewhere without you
   to the end of an endless belt, to be disposed of
      or given to the poor. A woman is smiling
into your face, urging you to get moving
   into the lobby of the wrong hotel
      with the heat turned off. She's giving you
a piece of plastic, one of those new keys
   that never work, yet you're supposed to work it
      on the right floor, in the right hallway,
in front of perfect strangers watching you,
   expecting you to be perfect, in the right door
      of the right room where you can't possibly sleep.

Being Taken for a Ride

They don't mean any harm. They're helping you
    get in, all the way in. They're making sure
      your legs are adjusted, your belt snapped,
with no loose ends sticking out to be caught
    when the door slams shut. And then they slam it
      and latch it. You see someone you don't know
already in the driver's seat, impatient with you,
    gunning the engine. The others are in the back,
      and you all move forward now into the street,
going somewhere. The driver holds the wheel
    too loosely with the fingers of one hand,
      one elbow out in the wind, his shaded eyes
not on the road, but on other drivers
    or himself in the mirror. You hate to say anything
      critical. After all, it isn't your car,
not even, really, your idea
    to be doing this, but everything is going
      much too fast and happening too fast,
and that strange music on the radio
    is too loud. After all, there are limits.
      Driving a car is a privilege. You can remember
driving your father's car inside the garage
    at night with the lights off and no key
      to turn the ignition on and no license
of your own yet. But even back then,
    you had a feeling for the road ahead
      ahead of time, of the You you were going to be.
Yet here you are, right now, afraid
    to speak your mind, buckled and locked
      in a passenger seat and being taken somewhere.

The Driver

It's a safe car. It belongs to somebody else,
    and you're parked legally near the right doorway,
        and you've made sure there's a tank of gas
and the engine's running okay. You're going to sit here
    as if you were supposed to sit here, which
        you are, minding your own business. You expect
others to do likewise. Your driver's license
    at first glance looks pretty much like you,
        and when the others, dressed like customers,
come out of the bank, they'll climb in by themselves
    and handle everything they're carrying
        by themselves, and as soon as all their shoes
are off the pavement, you'll go. You've got the route
    all picked out. You know where to turn,
        where to go fast, where you have to slow down
and drive like a tourist. But now the fat old lady
    in a twenty-year-old Lincoln is backing in
        ahead of you, lurching, half-clutching,
half-braking a foot at a time, and stalling it
    two feet from the curb, and a hotel limo
        is double-parking, almost touching your street-side,
unloading baggage, and a kid in an orange Edsel
    is jamming in back of you, half in a bus zone,
        and bailing out on an errand, and a cop
is resting his pale-blue elbow on the roof
    of the passenger side and looking in at you
        as the others scramble out of the door behind him,
and the cop says, smiling and nodding, *You guys kill me*
    and strolls away while they take their time deciding
        whose turn it is to sit in the jump seat,

who gets the outside windows, who gets to choose
    the first CD, and the lady in the Lincoln
        steps on the wrong pedal and goes zooming
a half a block. The limo glides after her.
    A City Transit tow truck has its hook
        under the Edsel and is hauling it off,
and as you drive away under the limit
    the tall buildings on each side of the street
        grow even taller, and ticker tape and confetti
come spilling down around you. Crowds on the curbs
    are cheering as loud as sirens. You raise the roof
        so the guys in back can stand up and enjoy it
out in the open, right in the sunshine,
    waving and grinning, taking green handfuls
        out of their satchels and tossing them up for grabs.

The Follower

The car ahead of you
is beautiful, so exactly
   what you'd imagined
   driving, you feel as proud
as if you were in it passing
people with no cars,
   who stand on the curbs of corners,
   watching, but not feeling
what you feel on the road
with the Car of Cars. It's moving
   forward, gliding at ease,
   power under its hood. Other cars
in other lanes or at crossings
are signaling this way,
   that way, blinking. It drives
   ahead without turning lights,
and when you blink, the Car
is splotches of olive-drab
   and is losing its outline
   against dead grass and leaves
beyond the shoulder, becoming
harder to follow, weaving
   and slowing down. You're conscious
   of following an order
of some importance
you can't understand. Now
   the Car is fading to black,
   dead black, is slowing
to a crawl. In a burst of lights
in an explosive rainbow
   of music, in outbursts
   of whistling steam steam-whistling

under stars, you see
a calliope leading the way.
      You pretend to steer. You're being
      guided. You're almost as strong,
almost as wonderful
as the cage bars around you.

At the Scene of Another Crime

We close the entrance and step carefully
and lightly here. We put on gloves
and sanitize ourselves. We're going to perform
an operation conducted like the music
being transmuted over the soft-speakers
through every corridor of a hospital.

We've sworn an oath: the body of this death
will be treated patiently, with orderly care.
We touch it now. We take its temperature.
We analyze its locale, its terminal posture.
We take its picture from our point of view.
We wrap it up. We put ourselves in its place.

Stakeout

You stand on the curb. You're waiting for the light.
You can see the door on the far side of the street.
Behind it, the others are waiting at a table,
one chair empty. You should be on time.

But a man's reading a tabloid under an awning.
Another in a hard hat sits by a sewer,
trying to act busy. At a shop window
a young woman pauses, her back turned,
not looking at dresses or her own reflection,
but at yours. The light has changed. Beside you,
a young man moves ahead. He's crossing the street,
but stops halfway. He glances back at you,
and suddenly with your left foot in the gutter
you're a character in a play you haven't rehearsed.
Everybody has business except you.

You're the only one who might do anything different,
so you do it. You put your hand over your mouth.
You glance overhead at nothing. You turn around
and hurry back because you've forgotten something.

Changing Rooms

You pull the curtain aside and edge your way,
    shoeless, out of the dressing room, one hand
        holding up (by the slack at the belt-line
where there's no belt) a pair of slacks
    (which don't belong to you), through a corridor,
        not quite caught in the act (but almost),
looking for some way out before the police
    block all the doors, or the loud husbands, wives,
        or private dicks come running toward you
out of old comedies, or the interrogator
    invites you to join him under the ceiling light
        to rehearse your answers. You shuffle forward
as if you'd been called too urgently in or out
    of the wrong bedroom. You face the front-view-
        and-both-profiles mirror. You stand as tall
and steady as you can while a woman kneels,
    touches the upper hump of the arch of your foot
        and with the upper hump of her other hand, the peak
of the vault of your inmost inner-seam. You take
    your numbers, your chalk marks, and your old straight lines
        with you in and out of the changing rooms.

In the Dark Room

The images begin to gather
under what looks like water.

You know what they'll be
because you half recall

what you thought you saw
and wanted to remember,

but the truth in black and white
grows gradually clearer

and finally stiffens
into what you feel you've known

all along was going to happen
in a time already gone

except for the negative
of memory. You stand there

and say to yourself, That's not
what I saw. That couldn't be all

I remember. It's only a blur
of what I couldn't see through.

I'll never know what it is,
let alone what it's going to be

though I squint and stare at it,
neutralized, hung out to dry.

6

What the Houses Were Like Then

You could stand outside of one on a paved street
and look at it and say it was your house.
You could go to the door and open it with a key
and take two steps and close it behind you.

You'd be inside then. You could stay inside
almost as long as you felt like. Nobody else
came in unless you said so. Hot or cold
water came out of pipes when you wanted it

and stopped when you didn't. There were two rooms
where you could eat when you needed to eat food.
There was only one basement. If you had to see
what was outside, you looked through a glass window

or pulled a curtain across and didn't think
about the clouds or what fell out of them.
Because of walls and ceilings, you could tell
your house was ending short of somebody else's.

Man Overboard

The moment you see him fall, you have to believe
    you're the only one who knows where he is now
        and you have to throw immediately after him
anything lighter than water, anything
    but yourself. No matter how strong a swimmer
        you think you are, you stay on board
and shout two crucial words over and over
    and fix your eyes on whatever is still floating
        and never, not for a single distracted second,
lose sight of it. No matter what happens now, no matter
    who else is shouting, no matter who
        may be yelling questions at you, standing beside you
or in front of you, commanding you to obey
    orders, to do something else, you keep your eyes
        on that one place where someone like you is trying
as hard and as long as possible not to be left
    alone, to be lost at sea. Your ship may be turning
        and heeling, slewing and interfering
with your line of sight like the shiftless waves themselves
    baffling each other, crossing each other, rising
        and falling for no reason, careless of whether
something like you can remember long enough
    why you're shouting, why you're trying to stare
        in what you have to believe is the right direction,
and you keep hoping, obeying only yourself
    till he's back on board (breathing or out of breath)
        or there's nothing left to point at or hope for.

Moving through Smoke

You'll feel tempted to run.
You must not run.
You should kneel and lie down
on the floor, the one place
where you can still breathe
something like air. Everything
over and under you
may collapse and burn
at any moment. To avoid
collapsing and burning too,
you should move
at a steady crawl
past door after door
without opening even
one because fire
may be behind it, ready
and able to come along
with you, ahead of you,
to wait for you at the end
of your passageway. Exit
then onto the stairs
on your good hands and knees
or your belly. Let gravity
take you step by step
rapidly down and out,
and if you're still alive
in clearer air, you should stand
and take a long look back
at what you almost were.

Unarmed Combat

You must think of yourself
and your body parts
    as weapons and loved ones
    at the same time, holding
each one dear, but ready
to do harm. Your hands
    and feet, those deadly ends
    of levers, can all four
reach the climax
of their surprising actions
    at the greatest possible distance
    from your vital organs
and your brain. They should form
the bases, perimeters,
    and parameters of all offensive/
    defensive positions, must be
the roots and branches
of your life. They can kill
    easily almost anything
    near enough to receive
the full impact
of what you've learned
    to give. But if your opponent
    (the word still means *the one*
opposite you) has stayed
remote, out of reach, and proves
    to have deadly arms, you must choose
    among moving forward

or backward slowly
or quickly, or of nearly
    suicidal attack or running away
    or of standing where you are
with eyes and ears open, your lips
rehearsing surrender.

Attention

Your heels together,
your feet fixed
at a half right-angle,
your whole body
erect, both shoulders
squared above the arch
of your chest, your arms
dangling without stiffness,
your digits relaxed,
your thumbs touching
your pant seams, eyes
on the level, aimed
unfocused straight ahead
at nothing, showing no sign
of recognition of
anything up close
which may be someone
in power, demanding
more attention,
inspecting you now
from ears to cheeks, from hair
to buckle, from crease
to shine, judging
you, dismissing you.

At Ease

You lower your shoulders now. You focus your eyes
    near or far. You turn them in any direction
        as long as your right foot stays where it is
and was when you were brought to your attention.
    It marks the spot, the fixed leg of your compass,
        with which you define your small perimeter
(with you inside). Here you may exercise
    unusual freedoms: to take your hands away
        from your upper thighs and make them into fists
with nothing in them, to move them somewhere else,
    to listen to marching music, to think your own thoughts,
        to hold your own opinions and keep them
to yourself. You will see others dressed like you
    in similar positions on all sides, all going through
        the motions of being at ease. You fight the temptation
to speak to them, to joke with them. All names
    are improper now. Your mouth is for breathing.
        Too long a meeting of eyes is disorderly conduct.

Under Fire

Because you heard the shot,
you know you're still alive, and so
    you have to decide now
    (not later on)
whether to fall down
or duck and run,
    but if you're near cover,
    go for it flat out
and stay there till you know
who, where, and how far
    and if you haven't been hit,
    fall anyway. Lie still.
No, lie still. And don't look.
You're going to have to think
    about how to be dead
    because someone's watching you
or at least your head or your heart
at the base of a steel notch
    or on a cross through glass,
    deciding what to do next,
which will depend on you,
on whether you move your hand
    or foot or open your eyes,
    on what you make of yourself
and how long it's going to take
and what you have in mind.

Night Reconnaissance

Though that hand in front of your face
in disputed territory
at night may be your own,
you should always remember
there are degrees of darkness.

If you crouch and lie down
and crawl from cover to cover,
from bushes to shadows of trees,
from a fence to a house to a door,
you shouldn't feel secure.

Others have been here
exactly where you are
and have used the same concealment.
They may be waiting for you,
may be looking at you
from a place darker than yours.

You have three tactical choices:
one, to retire in good order,
trusting your silhouette
will seem a less and less
inviting target, or two,
to go to ground and stay
there, hoping the dawn
will level the playing field
and redistribute light
to your advantage, or three,
to charge, your eyes wide open,
toward an enemy
you hope won't even be there.

The Stand-up Cell

A prisoner would sit down
    inside it if he could,
or kneel, even if it meant
    he was ready to pray
to the wrong god this time
    and was giving up
everything on his knees,
    but there's no room
for those knees to give in,
    to bend or buckle now
but against something upright,
    no room for his arms
to spread, nothing to hold
    onto or brace against
or embrace but bare walls,
    no hands left, no right
feet under the body
    lolling, no longer even
dreaming of lying down,
    the center of gravity
in both hips like a fire
    wanting to fall as far
as that other fire, but here
    unable to turn
or sink as far as sleep.

What the Stones Say

It isn't written in stone,
we say, meaning we'll change
our minds, maybe, if others
would just change theirs a little
on that slippery, unyielding ground
on the other side of the table.

Our fathers, long before us,
before they thought up how
to make words permanent,
before the alphabet,
chiseled out pictographs
and dabbled in graffiti.

And archaeologists tell us,
in chronological order,
these shapes were in their minds,
these shapes went down on stone:
first, solar discs, the sun
hard at the heart of being.

Then labyrinths, the strange
pathways to the gods.
Next, forms of rigid order,
geometrical designs.
Then people facing one way
on their knees, praying together.

Weapons of war and the hunt—
knives, crude spears, and arrows—
came next. Then houses and plots,
ceremonies of cults,
sketches of massacres,
and men mating with beasts.

On First Looking through the Wrong End of a Telescope

We aim it at the heavens, but vice versa
it shows us just how little the gods see
if they look back: a round ball behind glasses
with one gelatinous homemade lens exposing
an extremely nervous system lying wide open
to vague reflections, a rearrangement of dust
ready to shut down in the blink of an eye.

The Center of Gravity

It's somewhere between your hips.
    To haul your body
up out of a chair, you have to move
    that point over a line
between your feet by bending
    forward, cantilevering
your torso from both shoulders,
    scuffling your shoes
backwards, and then rising
    to this new occasion
and trying to stand there
    (if you simply want to stand
still in the same place,
    keeping your balance),
the whole point being the point
    must remain steady above
a baseline between your feet
    because if your back is up
against a wall with no room
    for maneuvering your arms,
you'll find your stubborn center
    of gravity won't quite make it
possible to stoop
    or change that one position
or direction without falling.

An Old Man Sitting Down

It may not be easy shaping yourself halfway
    between standing and lying down. You need
to focus, need something firm and level made
    for someone like you, trustworthy one more time,
staying where it belongs, keeping its shape
    right there, while you turn your back on it
during that hesitant, necessary, uncertain
    daring moment of giving in at the knees,
making it brace its own legs to remain
    supportive, confirming your physical self
as being acceptable, as being able
    after the fact to smile around at others,
to be, as at less critical times, once more
    almost at ease in your own eyes and in theirs.

An Old Man Stacking Firewood

His axe goes up and around
and down, quartering alder.

The haft of the axe was once
a branch of that same wood.

The chopping block is a stump.
The stack is the shade of blood.

One splits like the crackle of fire.
He leans against a trunk

whose lichen-covered bark
is the color of old bones.

What's left of his breath is warming
the gnarled roots of his fingers.

The Old Men

Old men are drunk with time.
—Emerson, *Journal*

There is so much of time
        to remember now wherever
they look, they find more
        and more not there where it was,
where they once were,
        and to the young they seem
drunk, incapable of being
        cold sober at the doors
of some old houses,
        at the gates of old gardens,
or on almost any shore.

The Hero

He's lying in the middle of a field,
his body humming with flies. In his hand, a broadsword

eaten by rust. On the dead grass beside him,
a breastplate, once embossed with pectorals,

now dented nearly as flat as the twisted wings
on his bronze helmet. His face, clenched like a fist,

still grapples for life, no matter how many times
the weather puts new masks on what he was.

Near the open mouth of the pouch strapped to his waist,
a mirror, a key, a dried mouse, and a stone.

7

The Eve of the Festival of Venus

(the anonymous Latin poem *Pervigilium Veneris,*
third or fourth century A.D.)

Tomorrow, love for the loveless, and for those already loved: more love.
Spring is new and is singing now. Spring is the world born again.
In spring birds mate once more, all lovers agree,
and the trees let down their bridal veils in the rain.
Tomorrow, love for the loveless, and for those already loved: more love.

Tomorrow, the matchmaker among the shadows of branches
will weave her myrtle arbors. At tomorrow's festival
she will lead us into the singing woods. Tomorrow, Venus
herself from her high throne will utter the only laws.
Tomorrow, love for the loveless, and for those already loved: more love.

Tomorrow, even the timeless air will ravish itself,
and under those showers and from the bubbling sea-foam
among green throngs and dashing fish-tailed horses,
wrapped in her flowing veils, Venus will be reborn.
Tomorrow, love for the loveless, and for those already loved: more love.

She herself colors the year crimson with gemlike flowers.
Herself under the breath of the west wind coaxes forth
the clusters of warm buds. Herself lets fall the dew
glittering against them from the passage of night air.
Tomorrow, love for the loveless, and for those already loved: more love

The tiny beads of dew distilled from the stars
on the clearest of nights are quivering, gathering
to spill in heavier drops, to fall and unfold
the virginal buds from their sheaths at the break of day.
Tomorrow, love for the loveless, and for those already loved: more love.

Look, the young flowers are flushing more and more deeply,
like small flares, like nipples rising from glowing breasts.
Herself has called the rose-vines to open those petals
like naked, virginal brides at the first morning.
Tomorrow, love for the loveless, and for those already loved: more love.

In a blend of the kiss of Cupid and the blood of Venus,
of firelight and jewels and the pulsing scarlet of sunrise,
tomorrow the bride, unashamed, will kindle blushes
on her breasts and her moist thighs like candle flames.
Tomorrow, love for the loveless, and for those already loved: more love.

The Goddess has told the nymphs to go to the myrtle bower.
Cupid goes with them, but never suppose that boy
will follow strict rules by bringing along his arrows.
Go, nymphs: he has cast away those shafts for a holiday.
Tomorrow, love for the loveless, and for those already loved: more love.

Venus has told him to go unarmed and stripped to the skin
in order to harm no lover with weapon or fire,
but be careful, nymphs: with his bow and his arrows gone,
he has nothing to cover himself, and Cupid is beautiful.
Tomorrow, love for the loveless, and for those already loved: more love.

Now Venus will offer maidens as innocent in love
as she once was while we all beg her, "Virgin of Delos,
don't interfere. Don't let our new-sprung flowers
be shadowed and stained by the slaughter of wild creatures."
Tomorrow, love for the loveless, and for those already loved: more love.

Venus herself will ask us to change our rules.
Venus herself will be calling us, beckoning us
for three long nights to join in the multitude
making their festival in the groves and gardens.
Tomorrow, love for the loveless, and for those already loved: more love.

There in those myrtle bowers, covered with garlands,
ravishing Ceres and Bacchus, her ravisher,
will perform for the god of poets, and tender Night
will be kept awake with singing. Venus will blame no one.
Tomorrow, love for the loveless, and for those already loved: more love.

Venus will preside in her judgment seat among flowers,
and her least word shall be law. The Graces
will lounge beside her, dressed with the blossoms
of a whole year's abundance from the plain of Enna.
Tomorrow, love for the loveless, and for those already loved: more love.

Virgins from the hills and forests, virgins from the farms,
virgins from shadowy, spring-fed grottos
tomorrow will lie down naked at the feet
of Venus who will forbid all marriage vows.
Tomorrow, love for the loveless, and for those already loved: more love.

Out of the clouds of spring to quicken the year
the rain will fall like a bridegroom into the lap
of his lovely bride. He will be passing
through the sky, through the sea, through everything on earth.
Tomorrow, love for the loveless, and for those already loved: more love.

Venus has hidden her body inside our bodies.
As wild as she made Trojans among the Latins
and the lusty sons of Romulus among the Sabines,
she will hold sway over our flesh and spirits.
Tomorrow, love for the loveless, and for those already loved: more love.

In a tide of desire, Venus will come pouring
down from the sky, through air and the sea
and the willing earth, through all our passageways.
She will teach us how to give birth to her again.
Tomorrow, love for the loveless, and for those already loved: more love.

She once gave a bride to her son and a bride to Mars,
and they in turn gave birth to Ramnes and Quirites,
and Romulus and Caesar followed, and all their children
and their children's children have prepared the way for us.
Tomorrow, love for the loveless, and for those already loved: more love.

Around us the whole countryside is trembling
for our delight and, look, the child of Venus, Love,
has been reborn among these flowering vines.
He touches her breast. He kisses her breast again.
Tomorrow, love for the loveless, and for those already loved: more love.

Look at the great bulls brushing their flanks against bushes!
The people are gathering. They are finding each other.
They come together as if they were being married. Listen:
birds sing in the shade, and sheep call to the rams.
Tomorrow, love for the loveless, and for those already loved: more love.

And now the pairs of hoarse-throated trumpeting swans
splash over the pools, and even the maid of Tereus
(who is really complaining about her indifferent husband
under a poplar tree) seems to be singing him love songs.
Tomorrow, love for the loveless, and for those already loved: more love.

She sings, but now I will be silent. Though everything else
and everyone else is singing, though silence is death,
I stand here mute. Though Apollo and my muse ignore me,
my song may come flying back to me like a swallow
tomorrow. Love for the loveless, and for those already loved: more love.

8

Between Neighbors

The complainant is a big man
    in his own goddamn front yard
        in a wheelchair, his voice as high
and highly offended (but only half
    as loud) as the dogs barking
        on his porch. His goddamn neighbors
(a young male couple
    standing their own ground
        deadpanned, on the other side
of the chain-link fence) went and aimed
    their hose at his expensive bird
        and hosed it. It was innocently
catching a little healthy goddamn sun
    in its cage. The cop bends close
        to listen. Then he walks off
to consult the complainees
    who say the barking, the barking goes
        on and on till they can't, just can't
stand it. If they pass on the sidewalk,
    the dogs bark. If they decide to swing
        on their porch swing, the dogs
bark, so, yes, they hosed his parrot
    and would do it again. The big man says
        between barks he needs, listen, he needs
the dogs as a signal to tell him
    strangers are nearby. The cop explains
        loudly the definition of *nuisance,*
issues a warning, turns his palms
    like a double stop sign up and against
        opposing sides, then demonstrates

keeping the peace by bending
    forward and saying, "Polly,
        want a cracker?" and offering
through the cage bars, one healing finger,
    and the wet-backed, green-backed,
        red-white-and-blue para-
military macaw gives a counterdemonstration
    to all of them of what can happen
        if you give somebody, anybody, the finger.

On Deck

My neighbors have gone overboard
with a cocktail party, and I'm trying to enjoy it
from over here in the dark like the helmsman
on an empty cruise ship, watching a full one pass.

Some of the guests are strolling out on deck
to share their drinks with the night, to breathe
and lean over the rail and point
at other points of view, islands of light
in other suburbs, to gaze at the sky
and guess at the names of stars and constellations,
none of which are where they're supposed to be.

A few of the passengers are side by side,
their silhouettes not quite touching,
whispering at the beginning or maybe the end
of a rite of passage. Someone is hugging someone.
A bottle breaks. Someone is laughing.
Someone is crying out loud
in a new language. Someone is taking a leak
over the side. Someone is throwing punches,
and somebody goddamn it is being sick
on the way back to the mess hall.

As I take over the watch, the groggy moths
have gathered to drink their share of the evening
at the only running light,
a blue fluorescent crackling insect-zapper.

Fighting the Blizzard

—police jargon for being drunk

A homeless drinking man
    trying to go somewhere
like home at night will take
    his first step
in one or two of the four
    official directions
and his second
    toward almost anywhere
but the first and the third
    and eventually will establish
a kind of balance
    among opposing forces
while he starts looking for work
    in a vestibule or doorway
or Dumpster or unlocked car
    or wherever enough dead leaves
can be heaped into a bed
    without breakfast,
and there he is, reexploring
    the unknown, still knowing not
to fight with an old blizzard
    but to take the enduring way
which is stopping, making a house
    out of the blizzard itself
or a cave into a drift
    to sleep before he's lost.

What Billy Graham Said to Me at the Fair

My editor said I should cover Billy Graham,
and I was the first reporter up against
the door of his Cadillac, the first one
to look him in both blue eyes and see his hair
and all sides of his smile. He had more teeth
than you might think. And he looked good. He looked
better than good. He looked like he believed
in looking even better. He looked like he'd been
unanimously reelected. He was wearing
a blue suit that would have no other gods
before it or after it. He greeted the others
of his persuasion appearing out of nowhere
by bending his head slightly and listening
as they pronounced their names in his right ear.

When he met the press, he answered a few questions
politely and somberly, and I raised my hand
like a pupil, like someone needing to be chosen.
Have you ever, I asked, *said anything in public
you regretted later?* He looked at me for a while
more in pity than sorrow. *I don't think
that's a proper subject for discussion,* he said.

In the Emergency Room

He won't do it he won't let them
   do hardly any more
      than look at that place
in his throat if we don't operate
   tonight a simple procedure
      no or else no your throat goes
shut you won't breathe old man
   when you're dead but no
      he won't do it he knew
somebody once who let them do it
   who never talked or walked
      again you're going
to die so what
   so's everybody else he'll take
      his chances but you don't
have to it's easy it's like
   no not very pleasant choking
      no to death you won't
enjoy it in the worst way
   no you think it's hard
      breathing now you wait
a few more hours if you last
   that long you'll find
      out all you want to know
about breathing no like the wind
   knocked out of you shaking
      his head we have to go
in there immediately or else
   no all over before
      you know it you don't

realize what's happening
    no like falling sort of asleep a nap
      you wake up better but how
does he know he'll wake up at all
    if he signs his name on this form
      that says we can
do it no you don't even have to
    sign it just say yes no yes
      no he doesn't think it's necessary
it is it isn't why am I
    doing this for the fun of it just nod
      so somebody else can see you'll save
your life tonight right now all
    right did you say all right he says
      all right it's yes he said it did
you hear him say it's all right again
    is it all right say it out loud he says all right
      all right all right do it.

Weeds

A weed is a plant out of place.
—Edwin Rollin Spencer, *All about Weeds*

They want to look as if they belonged in a garden.
They sprout in flowerbeds and have leaves like flowers.
Most are too tall too soon. Their blossoms
lead short lives, and their seeds scatter
in all directions and grow up out of place,
out of order, some of them out of sight,
going underground, sending out creepers
to check out territory, playing it safe,
staying away from dangerous daylight.

They claim the ends of streets where they take over
places always for sale. They grow there.
Some of them do. They fight it out.
Some, only a few, are poisonous.
The toughest ones have acid fruit and thorns.

An Informal Elegy for Neckties

Many still hang in closets, bearing the signs
of a thousand and one immemorial knots
or in folds of tissue paper in narrow boxes
on shelves or in shut drawers, never to be exposed
under the chins of men in photographs
who are no longer with us, who have grown even more rigid
like mediums demonstrating manifestations of ectoplasm
or like drunks in the act of redecorating their own shirtfronts.

No matter what their designs and configurations—polite geometry,
four-square tartans, old school diagonals, bilateral disagreements,
attempts at monochromatic subtlety, insignias of family curses,
chaos—they have reached a common end.

The authorities in charge of disappointment and isolation
have always taken them away from prisoners.

Looking Respectable

Beware of all enterprises that require new clothes.
—Thoreau

What are you up to now? You're here at the center
of what is probably your whole attention
trying to put on the dog for an enterprise
you know as well as the next man isn't you.

You're going to be an adjunct, not of your own,
but of an official body, to give what you thought
was you into the hands of people who don't
want you to be whoever that was you were.

You look as if you're dreaming of doing something
you don't know how to do, but are going to do it
any old way and suffer the consequences
of being in step, in style, in uniform.

You're modeling some kind of new behavior.
What now appears as you in a tailor's mirror
(two sidelong others outflanking the little left
and right of your front view) looks underemployed.

Doing Six Impossible Things before Breakfast

I remembered where I was.
I remembered who I was. I recognized
the meaning of three small luminous numbers.
I remembered why
I had to get out of bed. I got out of bed.
I remembered why I had to walk down the stairs.

What to Do All Day

You can seize it, but you feel it
slipping between your fingers,
    and although perpetual prayer
    is difficult to maintain
while you do good works
and have second thoughts,
    you can seize it again and look
    on the bright side as a form
of personal entertainment
like remembering your maker
    or reenacting your more
    successful un-Christian endeavors
to please those surrounding you
who need to be pleased. You may devote
    moments to self-cleansing,
    to collecting and freshening
old grievances or puzzling over
the mysteries of the obvious
    or may come to the aid
    of the poor in spirit
or heal the sick or rehearse
the most common errors
    of your superiors or simply
    stop, listen, and look
at almost anything
chancing your way at sundown
    and may take your reward
    for granted, may make your bed,
lie in it, and know you've wasted
precious little time.

Thoreau and the Quagmire

His boots would sink there, down where they belonged
   in the muddy water, on the dead and newly born
      jumble of life. He wanted to know and feel
what hadn't come to light yet, what might be keeping
   its darkness to itself in what the townsmen,
      even his good neighbors, were calling *waste land.*
Among those hummocks and through the ponds between them,
   he touched in the open air and with both hands
      the roots, the sprouts and stems, the unfolding leaves
and spikelets and, with both his feet in the muck,
   found where they began. He said their names
      over and over to himself. But he hardly knew
what to do with those same hands and feet
   in the houses of strangers. They would search for each other
      nervously at his knees or between them or forget
the way into pockets. His backward or forward feet
   might lose their places, might stagger him
      on carpets or polished hardwood, might make him lurch
off-balance, might seat him awkwardly
   in the quagmire of a chair, with a host and hostess
      talking and listening. He would try his best
to pay his respects by meeting their painful price
   of time and attention, hoping they might be as rich
      as purslane, target weed, or evergreen lambkill.

At the Deep End of the Public Pool

These people in the water
are no longer themselves
    but are feeling much more
    buoyant, more aware of
and obedient to the laws
of heat exchange and momentum
    and the motives of bare hands
    at the ends of arms
and feet at the ends of legs.
They have almost nowhere
    to go, but are going
    anyway. Those who can float
are giving in and up
to the oldest of sensations
    near a surface so transparently
    manageable, they don't need
to think about trusting it
to be where it was. This liquid
    stays in its place, regardless
    of how many strangers try
to make it private, to gather it
and keep it all to themselves.

In the Graveyard of Major Appliances

Among the boxcar wheels and the flattened cars
up against the jungles of rusty pipes
and the cat's cradles of rebars, they look outstanding
in the steel mill scrap yard under the slow rain.

They are its only whiteness—refrigerators,
stoves, washers, dryers, and thawed freezers.

They've been let go by housekeepers and cooks,
husbands and homemakers, but still maintain
their centers of power. Most have stayed upright.
The few that landed askew look stoic about it.

Though they're no longer making anything
hotter, colder, or cleaner, or being urged
to disobey the laws of thermodynamics
while running temperatures, this isn't the end.
They wait for the same old furnace and resurrection.

The Solution to Yesterday's Puzzle

We're showing you what you didn't understand
yesterday, couldn't make head or tail of,
the empty spaces you struggled and puzzled over,
what you should have known, remembered, or found out,
which all seem painfully clear now from One Across
to a larger number Down. All your good guesses
and tentative, blacked-out failures
have been cleansed of error, reduced in size,
and seem amusing enough for another day
of questions without answers.

Knots

Men had to learn to make them
    the hard way by losing
too much without them, the burdens
    they couldn't carry far enough
in their arms or lift or lower,
    what otherwise might run
or drift away or fall too far and be
    lost out of reach. The fibers twisted
into strands and the strands
    twisted, the bitter end
turned back and around
    and through, again
through, knots overcame
    even the weaknesses
of their own substance
    and could be made to join
each other or bring together
    what had been broken
by too much strain, to bind
    in a way that could be loosened
quickly or never loosened at all
    except by the unraveling
stroke of a sword or the later
    private touch of a hangman
or the light fingers grown clever
    at undoing a snarled love knot.

Cell Division

They didn't wake in the night. Night held them close
together, as always, in a single cell,

but the nervelike carriers they shared, those threads
that had made them one, were dissolving at their centers,

realigning, stretching, straightening, and withdrawing
into separate orders with nothing in between

the halves of love but a divisive membrane.

A Snap Quiz in Body Language

We can't hear what they're saying, but that man
is holding that woman in his arms. Your assignment
is to deduce their thoughts from what they do.
They've left no apparent space between their bodies.
It could be called a close embrace, but notice
her arms are at her sides, her hands relaxed,
her face impassive, while he's whispering
something in her ear. His upper torso
is tilted slightly forward. Hers is yielding
but not in a way suggesting sweet surrender.
Is this a seduction scene? Is she being held
for questioning? Should she call a lawyer?
He's looking into her eyes now. How wide open
would you say they are? What does he see in them?
If he were to let her go, class, what would she do?

For a Man Who Wrote *Cunt*
on a Motel Bathroom Mirror

You thought she was asleep. You were afraid
to hear what she'd call *you*
if you said it out loud as a parting shot
at the door, so you took the sneaky way out
and used her own lipstick against her, against the mirror
where you felt certain she'd look no later
than dawn, but would find, instead of herself
in there again behind glass, your blunt reflection,
your last word on the subject.

But I'm here to tell you she was wide awake.
Behind her eyelids she followed every move
of yours, the jingle of small change
when you finally found your pants, the smallest squeak
of your run-down heels in the bathroom,
the soft click of the latch.

She let out the breath she'd been holding and keeping
to herself, took a quick shower, considered
the small end of your vocabulary,
and taxied home. She didn't bother
erasing your word, but passed it on
as a kind of tip to the maid, who wouldn't clean up
after you either, but left it to the imagination
of another customer this cold morning,
who's passing it back to you.

Night Song from the Apartment Below

The argument begins. One voice is overcoming
another because it's had it, it's had enough
of all this shit and, unaccompanied, rises
to the edge of screaming and past it
till the column of air in that throat has nearly abandoned
everything under it. Only the vault of the forehead
and the bridge of the nose are left to resonate.

An abrupt pause. A brief intermission.

Lotte Lehmann, who knew all there was to know
about singing, said in the upper register
one should always have two notes in reserve
which one never uses.
                    And now the second voice
comes lurching up and out of the dungeon
beneath the memory of the other, from as deep
as the torture chamber of the diaphragm,
offering to surrender everything
imaginable, hope, wine, money, love,
credit cards, even the need to be touched.

In the following silence, the long silence,
those of us already lying down
in our own forms of darkness are listening
in the name of mercy for the next wrong note.

Desire

Flies are on the alert,
     even when posing
to groom their busy wings
     or clear some of those eyes,
so all frogs, because
     they have to, have to
know exactly what
     the tips of their tongues
should do to satisfy
     their natural desire
for a fuller life and stomach
     and have all proved it
through numberless generations
     of choristers and swarms
of good examples. Even if frogs
     are punished with a spark
or a slight touch of acid,
     they persist. They pay
the price and will keep on
     snapping flies in spite
of this new pain. Yet at last
     even these slow learners
master their desire. They try
     and try to forget. But no matter
what the curious minds
     in curious laboratories
have devised, no frog on earth
     or in water, from a spring
peeper, its tadpole tail
     only half gone,
to an old bullfrog
     under a lily pad,

can be the least bit
  tempted or forced to take
a fly sitting still, showing
  no sign of leaving
where it is or of moving even
  the least important part
of itself to a new position.
  All frogs would starve to death
among motionless flies.

The Spider's Eye

For love hath a spider's eye
To find out some appropriate pain.
—Yeats

All spiders have as many eyes
    as they have legs, but even the champion
of arachnids, the jumping spider,
    sees only a vague blur
beyond five inches
    and needs no painful webbing,
only a lifeline. What spiders hunger for
    as they wait at the still center
or the soft door they've spun
    out of themselves has left them
no way to admire the flutter
    of mothlike evasive behavior
or nuances of flight or baffling
    or baffled changes of direction
under the influence of the wind
    or the moon. What spiders feel
least must be the slightest impulse
    to give pain. True, they have jaws
with poison fangs, but their purpose
    is to take all pain away,
to deaden it, to welcome
    nearly blindly the fulfillment
of their first lifelong desire
    which is the same for lovers.

The Day I Believed in God

I don't believe
He knew ahead of time
which day it would be. He didn't
    foresee how far forward
    and backward I would lean
    on the edge of the cliff
to stay balanced and keep on
thinking of Him. The choice
had always been between
    the chaotic accidents
    called days and nights
    and the likelihood of a detectable confounding ceremony
involving vacuums and unaccountable stars. For countless hours
I had resisted the temptation to theorize
in the collapsible jittery unhinged abstract
    deliberate scrawny textures of Latinate scholarship
    because if He existed at all
    He was lost somewhere in that brittle jungle of dead sticks,
that wickerwork jackstraw wasteland, picky but pointless,
where hooded ecclesiastic scribblers and scratchers parted
and parsed with their backs turned on the lunacy of disbelievers
    and played host to themselves, the professional genitors
    and janitors of what they were supposed to believe in. God
    knows I believed in Him one day
but won't admit it. Those were grim hours,
all sleepless twenty-four of them,
when I believed malign indifference
    was my guiding light. He knows better
    than to say out loud or cause to be written down
    anything that might be

used against Him now, and why
should He? He has nothing
to gain but my allegiance
　　whose lack of substance
　　and general uselessness
　　(He should be well aware)
began even before sunrise
the very next morning when
I put Him back where He'd been.

A Congo Funeral

Once, when a good man died, his friends would dress him
like the king of a tribe no one had ever seen.
In a forest clearing, in a room without walls,
they would seat him in a chair, crown him with flowers,
and paint him. They would daub his forehead yellow,
his face white and pale-green, and all around him
they would mold, out of mud and clay, an audience
of smaller people and would paint them too,
and on the morning of the funeral
the villagers who came would pay a coin
to see this king who had acted out his life
among them, and then, in the dying evening,
they would leave him to be admired by the clay people
under the moon and the morning sun and rain
till all those shapes sank back to earth again.

David Wagoner is the author of eighteen
books of poems and ten novels, one of which,
The Escape Artist, was made into a movie by
Francis Ford Coppola. He has received an
American Academy of Arts and Letters award,
the Sherwood Anderson Award, the Fels Prize,
the Ruth Lilly Poetry Prize, six yearly prizes
from *Poetry,* and fellowships from the Ford
Foundation, the Guggenheim Foundation, and
the National Endowment for the Arts.
A former chancellor of the Academy of
American Poets, he was the editor of *Poetry
Northwest* from 1966 until its last issue in 2002.

Illinois Poetry Series

Laurence Lieberman, Editor

The Ways We Touch
Miller Williams (1997)

The Rooster Mask
Henry Hart (1998)

The Trouble-Making Finch
Len Roberts (1998)

Grazing
Ira Sadoff (1998)

Turn Thanks
Lorna Goodison (1999)

Traveling Light:
Collected and New Poems
David Wagoner (1999)

Some Jazz a While:
Collected Poems
Miller Williams (1999)

The Iron City
John Bensko (2000)

Songlines in Michaeltree: New and
Collected Poems
Michael S. Harper (2000)

Pursuit of a Wound
Sydney Lea (2000)

The Pebble: Old and New Poems
Mairi MacInnes (2000)

Chance Ransom
Kevin Stein (2000)

House of Poured-Out Waters
Jane Mead (2001)

The Silent Singer: New and Selected
Poems
Len Roberts (2001)

The Salt Hour
J. P. White (2001)

Guide to the Blue Tongue
Virgil Suárez (2002)

The House of Song
David Wagoner (2002)

X =
Stephen Berg (2002)

Arts of a Cold Sun
G. E. Murray (2003)

Barter
Ira Sadoff (2003)

The Hollow Log Lounge
R. T. Smith (2003)

In the Black Window: New and
Selected Poems
Michael Van Walleghen (2004)

A Deed to the Light
Jeanne Murray Walker (2004)

Controlling the Silver
Lorna Goodison (2005)

Good Morning and Good Night
David Wagoner (2005)

American Ghost Roses
Kevin Stein (2005)

Battles and Lullabies
Richard Michelson (2005)

Visiting Picasso
Jim Barnes (2006)

The Disappearing Trick
Len Roberts (2006)

Sleeping with the Moon
Colleen J. McElroy (2007)

Expectation Days
Sandra McPherson (2007)

Tongue & Groove
Stephen Cramer (2007)

A Map of the Night
David Wagoner (2008)

National Poetry Series

Eroding Witness
Nathaniel Mackey (1985)
Selected by Michael S. Harper

Palladium
Alice Fulton (1986)
Selected by Mark Strand

Cities in Motion
Sylvia Moss (1987)
Selected by Derek Walcott

The Hand of God and a Few
Bright Flowers
William Olsen (1988)
Selected by David Wagoner

The Great Bird of Love
Paul Zimmer (1989)
Selected by William Stafford

Stubborn
Roland Flint (1990)
Selected by Dave Smith

The Surface
Laura Mullen (1991)
Selected by C. K. Williams

The Dig
Lynn Emanuel (1992)
Selected by Gerald Stern

My Alexandria
Mark Doty (1993)
Selected by Philip Levine

The High Road to Taos
Martin Edmunds (1994)
Selected by Donald Hall

Theater of Animals
Samn Stockwell (1995)
Selected by Louise Glück

The Broken World
Marcus Cafagña (1996)
Selected by Yusef Komunyakaa

Nine Skies
A. V. Christie (1997)
Selected by Sandra McPherson

Lost Wax
Heather Ramsdell (1998)
Selected by James Tate

So Often the Pitcher Goes to Water
until It Breaks
Rigoberto González (1999)
Selected by Ai

Renunciation
Corey Marks (2000)
Selected by Philip Levine

Manderley
Rebecca Wolff (2001)
Selected by Robert Pinsky

Theory of Devolution
David Groff (2002)
Selected by Mark Doty

Rhythm and Booze
Julie Kane (2003)
Selected by Maxine Kumin

Shiva's Drum
Stephen Cramer (2004)
Selected by Grace Schulman

The Welcome
David Friedman (2005)
Selected by Stephen Dunn

Michelangelo's Seizure
Steve Gehrke (2006)
Selected by T. R. Hummer

Veil and Burn
Laurie Clements Lambeth (2006)
Selected by Maxine Kumin

Other Poetry Volumes

Local Men and Domains
James Whitehead (1987)

Her Soul beneath the Bone: Women's
Poetry on Breast Cancer
Edited by Leatrice Lifshitz (1988)

Days from a Dream Almanac
Dennis Tedlock (1990)

Working Classics: Poems on Industrial
Life
Edited by Peter Oresick and Nicholas
Coles (1990)

Hummers, Knucklers, and Slow
Curves: Contemporary Baseball Poems
Edited by Don Johnson (1991)

The Double Reckoning of Christopher
Columbus
Barbara Helfgott Hyett (1992)

Selected Poems
Jean Garrigue (1992)

New and Selected Poems, 1962–92
Laurence Lieberman (1993)

The Dig and Hotel Fiesta
Lynn Emanuel (1994)

For a Living: The Poetry of Work
Edited by Nicholas Coles and Peter
Oresick (1995)

The Tracks We Leave: Poems on
Endangered Wildlife of North America
Barbara Helfgott Hyett (1996)

Peasants Wake for Fellini's Casanova
and Other Poems
Andrea Zanzotto; edited and translated
by John P. Welle and Ruth Feldman;
drawings by Federico Fellini and Augusto
Murer (1997)

Moon in a Mason Jar and What My
Father Believed
Robert Wrigley (1997)

The Wild Card: Selected Poems, Early
and Late
Karl Shapiro; edited by Stanley Kunitz
and David Ignatow (1998)

Turtle, Swan and Bethlehem in Broad
Daylight
Mark Doty (2000)

Illinois Voices: An Anthology of
Twentieth-Century Poetry
Edited by Kevin Stein and G. E. Murray
(2001)

On a Wing of the Sun
Jim Barnes (3-volume reissue, 2001)

Poems
William Carlos Williams; introduction
by Virginia M. Wright-Peterson (2002)

Creole Echoes: The Francophone
Poetry of Nineteenth-Century
Louisiana
Translated by Norman R. Shapiro;
introduction and notes by M. Lynn Weiss
(2003)

Poetry from Sojourner: A Feminist
Anthology
Edited by Ruth Lepson with Lynne
Yamaguchi; introduction by Mary
Loeffelholz (2004)

Asian American Poetry: The Next
Generation
Edited by Victoria M. Chang; foreword
by Marilyn Chin (2004)

Papermill: Poems, 1927–35
Joseph Kalar; edited and with an
Introduction by Ted Genoways (2005)

The University of Illinois Press
is a founding member of the
Association of American University Presses.

Composed in 10.5/14 Adobe Garamond Pro
with Folio Bold display
at the University of Illinois Press
Designed by Dennis Roberts
Manufactured by Thomson-Shore, Inc.

University of Illinois Press
1325 South Oak Street
Champaign, IL 61820-6903
www.press.uillinois.edu